Kate Lorenc

MY CAMINO
A JOURNEY OF SELF-EXPLORATION

Title
MY CAMINO. A JOURNEY OF SELF-EXPLORATION.

Copyright © Katarzyna Lorenc, 2023
All rights reserved

Translated by
Tomasz Jurewicz

Designed by
Agnieszka Henclik, Katarzyna Kwiatkowska, Dominika Majchrowska

ISBN: 9798396815810

Published by

No part of this publication may be reproduced, stored in or introduced into retrieval system, or transmitted, in any form or by any means (electronic, mechanical, photocopying, recording or otherwise), without written permission the copyright owner. Requests for permission should be directed to klorenc@bizyou.pl.

Enjoy the journey!

TABLE OF CONTENTS

INTRODUCTION
9

1. PACKING
13

2. BOM CAMINHO
15

3. SHADOWS OF CASTLES ON THE SAND
18

4. MY PACE
21

5. MINISTRY OF STRANGE WALKS
24

6. ANGEL
27

7. RETURNING TO BALANCE
30

8. DISAPPEARING
34

9. CLOSE TO MYSELF
37

10. REST
40

11. UPHILL
43

12. VIVA LA FIESTA
46

13. STOPOVERS
50

14. UNLOADING THE BURDEN
53

15. FUNERAL AT THE END OF THE WORLD
56

16. CLAM
60

17. COMING BACK
64

18. ULTREIA!
67

19. SUMMARY
71

REVIEWS
73

ABOUT THE AUTHOR
80

INTRODUCTION

For some time it had been dawning on me that something was coming to an end in my life, both professionally and privately. It was like the feeling you get when you climb a ladder leaning against the wrong building. Despite my successes, the satisfaction was short-lived, or I could hardly feel it. I needed a change. My daily duties consumed so much time that I didn't have a moment to think: what next? I needed to reconnect with myself, but not on a superficial level, like when I was wondering what I wanted to eat. I needed the peace and quiet to understand myself again.

I had already introduced that in small doses as part of my morning routine, reserved just for myself. It included several small rituals that gave me space to reflect on myself and my life each day, outside of the flow of daily chores and commitments. That's how it started. Then I asked the team to clear my calendar for one month so I could go on holiday. I live with an agenda in my hand, all my activities are in it, all my time is scheduled, so getting it to be empty was no mean feat. In spite of the temptations - various attractive job offers came in - I managed to secure a month's empty space. I contemplated visiting a friend in Los Angeles or taking another trip to Cyprus with nice company. But it didn't work out. The dates didn't match. Communication was breaking down. One morning it dawned on me that maybe it could be time for me alone and...

Two days later I woke up convinced that it was time for my 'Camino'. A long time ago, a couple I met on a Lofoten cruise told me how they had walked all the way from France to Santiago de Compostela. A few years later I watched the film 'The Way'. But until that moment, I hadn't thought of going. And then? I was sure I would go. Later I learnt that it is known as 'the call' and many people on the trail had the same experience.

The next day, when I checked what the Camino and the main route really was, I almost fell off my chair. It turned out that the French route was 880 km long. I knew it wasn't for me. When I read more about it, I learnt there were more routes. I liked the Portuguese trail, to be precise – its coastal version with sunshine, lapping ocean and me. The most hedonistic version.

Start in Porto – 280 km to Santiago de Compostela and over 90 km to Fisterra. The place that the Spanish called the end of the world. That's all I needed! The end of the wrong version of my world. Waiting for my upgrade, I'll go just there!

To keep my family and loved ones from worrying about me travelling alone, I started to write posts. This book brings them together. As it turned out, a lot of people were walking with me. Accompanying and cheering me on, they asked themselves similar questions. Like me, they found their answers. Perhaps I can invite you too for a walk to get to know yourself. I hope that you'll find something important along this journey – like my Facebook friends and me. Something that has been there all the time, but has been pushed aside. It's time to put yourself back in the right place in your life.

I suggest you read one chapter a day, for example over your morning coffee and remember the questions so that you can write down your answers in the evening. You don't have to answer all of them, just the ones that matter most to you. It was my method. But do as you please, it's your Camino now.

> *Does the wanderer choose the road, or the road the wanderer?*
>
> **Garth Nix, Lirael**

PACKING

July 5, 2022

I'm taking myself on a date, running away into my inner world. I will walk over 400 km alone in 21 days. Naturally, this is an optimistic assumption. The route runs along the ocean, through the forest and back along the ocean. Sometimes something gets stuck in your head and you can't get it out. But so far, so good, I'm happy. Keep your fingers crossed.

I've bought a beautiful women's backpack (48 litres). I've read the blogs. I've made a list of everything I need and bought it all. I've talked to expert travellers. I've had a lesson in walking with poles. I'm ready for everything. Good preparation is the key to success.

- What is your reason to get on the road?
- What part of yourself do you want to discover?
- What will you put in your backpack?
- What kind of preparation will be enough for you to set out?

NOTES

2 BOM CAMINHO

July 7, 2022

I've made it and survived the first day

I still have no idea who Kate is without all her functions, titles, jobs, make-up and high heels, but here I am.

15 km with a 13 kg backpack is a lot for me for starters.

To get to my first destination from Porto, you could take the metro.

Last night I thought I wouldn't manage to get up for dinner, but today I'm fine. It looks like I'll 'turtle up' there, taking it step by step.

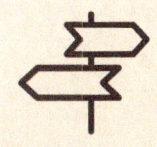

Porto – Matosinhos

DISTANCE 15 km
NUMBER OF STEPS 24,738

MY CAMINO. A JOURNEY OF SELF-EXPLORATION   15

Thank you for all your wishes and support. It's touching, and every now and then during the walk I'm overwhelmed with such tenderness that tears come to my eyes. I don't know yet what it's all about.

I got accosted by several people who wished me: **bom caminho**. An old lady in a café in Porto was the first to tell me this, adding that she wished me to find what I came for. I cried and she hugged me. I will never forget it. Many people smile when they see me. Fortunately, I can't see myself, so I assume it's out of kindness, rather than indulgence.

- What do your roles, functions, titles and positions mean to you today?
- When do they serve and when do they restrict you?
- Which ones do you identify with?
- Which have dominated you?
- What else can't you imagine yourself and your day without?
- What is holding you back?
- How would it feel to leave it for a while and see how it is different?
- Who would you most like to hear 'bom caminho' from?
- Whose wishes for a good journey would energize you the most?

NOTES

3 SHADOWS OF CASTLES ON THE SAND

July 8, 2022

I built a castle on the sand

My first cottage by the ocean. It won't last long. A wonderful sunset behind me. I would bet my life that the setting sun was shaped like a shell.

My knee began to hurt at night. I'm scared how quickly courage goes away when I'm in pain.

After a warm-up, things went rather well. I made 24,000 steps this morning. Here's my lesson learnt: **focusing on the goal is tiring**. It is easier if you listen to the waves or watch your steps. The goal is there to get you going, but then... I don't know. I'm sitting in artificial shade waiting for the heat to ease off.

The ocean as cold as... There is nothing to envy.

Hugs to you! Have a good journey!

> *The limits of what is possible are in your mind.*
> *The only walls that can stop you*
> *are the ones you build yourself.*

Author unknown

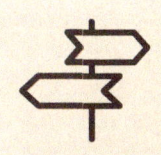

Labruge – Povoa de Varzim

DISTANCE 13 km
NUMBER OF STEPS 25,541

- What is your castle in the sand?
- What are you most afraid of seeing in yourself?
- What kind of self are you most afraid of?
- Are you building castles in the sand or solid constructions?
- What do you want to do with your fears?
- When does your courage falter?
- What limitations in discovering yourself do you see today?
- What's blocking you the most?

NOTES

4 MY PACE

July 10, 2022

Yesterday I was really dragging

I didn't sleep a wink in the alberga. I walked over 30,000 steps on an easy route in good company. Good conversation, nice time. However, with 7 km to go, my whole body was already aching. I found the nearest campsite, set up my tent and then hit the sack for a good 5 hours. I threw everything out of my backpack. Today, 45,000 steps over the hills, no big deal. Three differences: sleep, lighter backpack and walking at my own pace. I didn't change it even in the best company and I didn't lose strength. **When I change the pace because of others – I begin to fade**. These are my lessons learnt from the route to Viana do Castello. One third of the route behind me.

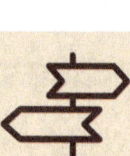

Povoa de Varzim – Apulia

DISTANCE 14,2 km
NUMBER OF STEPS 33,060

Apulia – Viana do Castelo

DISTANCE 32,4 km
NUMBER OF STEPS 45,433

- What sets the pace in your everyday life?
- What's your pace?
- What makes you change your pace?
- Who do you hold back your strength for?
- How do you want to take care of your pace?
- How can you communicate it to others in order to keep it?

MY CAMINO A JOURNEY OF SELF-EXPLORATION

NOTES

5 MINISTRY OF STRANGE WALKS

July 12, 2022

I thought I could walk

I can't. Yesterday I was learning to walk anew.

With each stop, my calves get stiffer and I can't move in a normal way. I set up my own Ministry of Strange Walks to find a way to relieve pain and tension: jumping, polka dancing, toe-to-heel swinging, shifting body weight from hip to hip, etc. It looked very strange, but I cracked the next 26 kilometres. No one will walk a Camino for you. I need to find my way, my own walk, probably more than one… You'll get support from the family de Santiago. They check if you are OK. Sometimes they stay with you a little longer, sometimes they smile and move on.

The best support I could give myself was trekking poles. They set the pace of my march. Supposedly, they scare off vipers and snakes. They help you climb uphill and stabilize you when you're going down. They become a part of me, harmonising the movement and distributing the weight. They help me keep a straight posture. I'd love to have such poles when I return to everyday life. Something that will accompany me on the road, will be mine, and will give me support. What will it be? I don't know yet.

Viana do Castelo – Caminha

DISTANCE 26,6 km
NUMBER OF STEPS 44,659

- What type of walk do you take through life?
- Which one do you want more of and which less?
- Which one will give you the balance and stamina for the long march?
- What's your posture?
- What's hurting you?
- Which part of your posture is responsible for that?
- Do you have your own poles for your daily walk through life?
- What are they?
- When do you take them with you and when do you leave them behind?

NOTES

6 ANGEL

July 13, 2022

I have an Angel

He arrived in Povoa de Varzim and now he's walking with me. The Angel massages my feet and calves, he offers to swap backpacks twice a day (his weighs 5 kg) and refills the wine. In short – a perfect Angel. He has his own pace, different from mine, and a very peculiar way of walking. He doesn't want me to change mine. Sometimes he comes closer, sometimes he stays further away. He gives me space, but he's also watching me closely. He asks a lot of questions, and seems genuinely interested in me. Walking at my own pace, I stayed a little ahead of him. I don't want him to miss his destination, but he said I'm part of his Camino and that's what it's all about. People are part of our journey. They bring us information and are a reflection of ourselves. A wonderful day behind me.

Caminha – Saõ Pedro da Torre

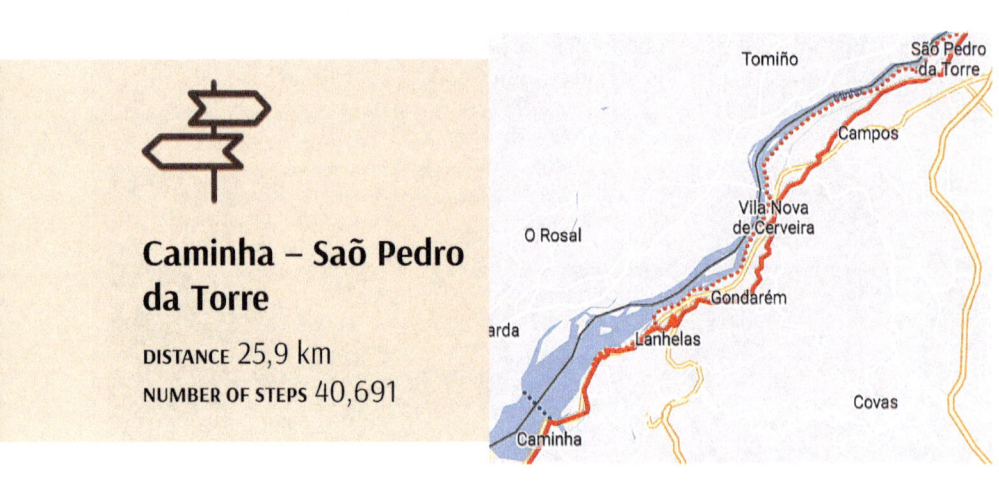

DISTANCE 25,9 km
NUMBER OF STEPS 40,691

- Do you have your angel in human form?
- What information have the angels brought you recently?
- Do you appreciate your angel?
- When did you last say to your angel: 'Thank you for being'?
- Who will you make room for on your journey?
- Who will you let walk beside you?
- What do you want to ask the angel for on your journey of self-exploration?

NOTES

7 RETURNING TO BALANCE

July 15, 2022

With 177 km behind me I still have 80 km to go to my first destination

I've never walked so much day after day. A great insight today. In the morning I had a pain in my left foot and right calf. I thought I would take ketonal to relieve the pain. But the Angel suggested finding a pace that would make the pain go away. First, I watched myself walk and noticed that my stronger right leg wanted to stretch as far forward as possible. Taking over too much weight, the left one was limping. When I curbed the ambitions of my right leg, the left stopped hurting, and then the right calf felt better. Next I tried to find front-to-back balance by aligning the body posture and adjusting the backpack as I went up and down the hill. Effect? It was fun to walk again. It probably wouldn't matter much in the short run. Eventually rest or massage would do the trick. But here quality translates into distance and health.

If I turned it into a metaphor and treated my right leg as if it was driven by the mind and the left leg by the heart or gut, it would mean that I could go further when I keep my ambitions in check and balance them out by leaving space to the heart. When I'm tired, the stronger side takes the upper hand and there is no space for feelings. Front-to-back balance would be my point of 'here and now' without looking to the future or dwelling on history...

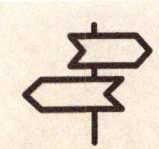

Saõ Pedro da Torre – O Porrino

DISTANCE 23,8 km
NUMBER OF STEPS 41,393

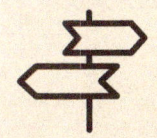

O Porrino – Arcade

DISTANCE 23,2 km
NUMBER OF STEPS 35,907

> *Life is like riding a bicycle.
> To keep your balance you must
> keep moving.*

Albert Einstein

- How is your balance?
- How do you want to balance your heart and mind?
- What issues are you looking forward to?
- What are the issues that keep you stuck in the past?
- How can you be here and now more often?
- What does it give you?
- What knocks you out of this state?

NOTES

8
DISAPPEARING

July 18, 2022

25 km left to Santiago

I could make it in one day, but no – today I will celebrate in Padron. I have two more lessons learnt. The day before yesterday I did 33 km in one day. It was too much. I wanted the Angel to walk as far as possible. We unnecessarily want things following others and for others. I was so sore and tired that I couldn't enjoy the evening. I disappeared. All this pressure I put on myself didn't make any sense. The magic that I was longing for didn't work until I decided to do short distances again, no matter what the Angel planned. I became part of the road, a tree, and the sun. And that's what I was going to be. It's wonderful to feel carefree, joyful and serene. Yesterday I swapped backpacks with the Angel. A lighter backpack is better. In mine, I have a lot of 'just-in-case' stuff. Unnecessarily. I find everything I need on the way.

I'll leave that 'just-in-case' thinking.

Have a good day, mates! Bon camiño!

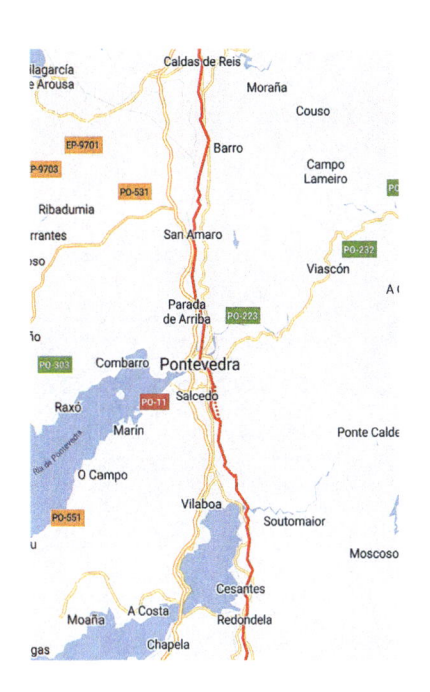

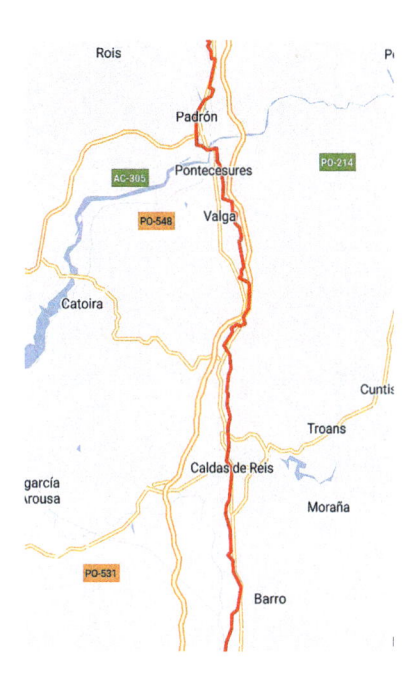

Arcade – Briallos

DISTANCE 29,7 km
NUMBER OF STEPS 51,641

Briallos – Pontecesures

DISTANCE 20,8 km
NUMBER OF STEPS 36,830

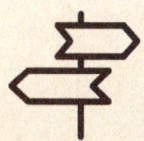

Pontecesures – Padron

DISTANCE 3,4 km
NUMBER OF STEPS 12,338

- What do you want for others and following others?
- What will help you stay focused on your journey?
- How can you meet others without giving up on yourself?
- When do you disappear for others?
- What about your backpack – what can you take out of it and leave?
- What pressure can you let go of today to enjoy your journey?

NOTES

9 CLOSE TO MYSELF

July 19, 2022

7 km away from Santiago

The Angel accomplished his mission and flew away. Walking uphill alone today. I'm enjoying my walk. Thoughts come and go one after another, like waves of emotions. I still feel as if I'm in open-heart surgery. I feel stronger, I don't hide my emotions, ordinary things can trigger a total avalanche. Also, conversations with my local family are getting more and more intense. They convey so much tenderness and space that I wish I could talk to my loved ones like this. But I can't yet. I'm afraid to open up so much. Maybe I shouldn't... I don't know. I feel safe in this shell of mine, but it's getting cramped too. Here I walk naked. I say what I feel, I feel it and it shows. Others can somehow cope with my tenderness, which normally scares me. My intention for the Camino was to be close to myself. I've never been any closer.

- When do you block your emotions?
- Why do you do that?
- What if you give space to your emotions?
- What if you have a better understanding of where they come from?
- What can you do to be with others and yourself in the energy of your heart?
- What do you need to change and what do you need to accept?
- What information is your body communicating now?
- What does it need to carry you and communicate with the world well?

It's not far, and the backpack is getting lighter every day. Hugs to you and to your intentions.

Grateful for the company of those who read and comment my posts, I took my written--down intentions to the star's garden (campus stella), and left them in the Cathedral. I would suggest you do the same with the intentions that you write down while reading my book – write them down, give them to your loved ones, take them to your 'place of force' and read them there. To a place where you feel good and reflective.

Padron – O Milladoiro

DISTANCE 17,6 km
NUMBER OF STEPS 30,572

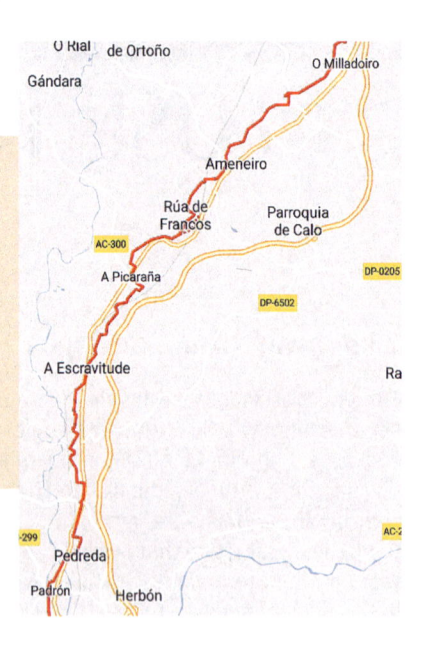

- What are your intentions for the road?
- What would be worth your camino?

MY CAMINO A JOURNEY OF SELF-EXPLORATION

NOTES

10 REST

July 20, 2022

I got up before dawn

I could not sleep. I walked down the first paths in the dark. All the paths led to my destination. At the stroke of eight, I entered the square in front of the cathedral almost alone. I was happy for your intentions. Thank you for your trust. I was honoured to carry them up the hill. Each got its candle and they were all read out to get where they need to go. Exchanging the sign of peace – such a touching moment at the mass for pilgrims. It is so important today to have peace within yourself. For me, it's time for a nap.

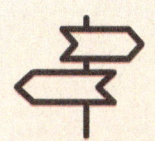

O Milladoiro – Santiago

DISTANCE 7,7 km
NUMBER OF STEPS 18,264

I'm leaving for Fisterra tomorrow. An extra 90 km to leave the stone I took from home there. I hope to say goodbye to everything that I no longer need along the way. I don't want excess baggage any more.

Are you moving on?

- How are you going to rest today?
  How will you take care of your inner peace?

NOTES

UPHILL

July 21, 2022

I'm no mountain goat

I don't like going uphill. It looks like physical exercise does not release my serotonin. 21 km today and the longest climb so far: 20-40 degree gradient for 6 km non-stop. A woman in front of me: 145 cm tall, 79 years old, she just jumped over Camino de nord, and ran on. Just don't compare yourself!!!

For sure, there are more women on the trail: young and very mature, walking solo and in pairs or trios.

Yesterday I said goodbye to my Camino Portuguese family. We had a wonderful time: performances of street artists, music, talking about our time together and their friends on the trail.

After this evening, I need to rethink how I build relationships. Those with my local family here were created by meeting and giving each other space where everyone could be themselves, in their own time and at their own pace. No adjusting, self-restraint or coercion. On a daily basis, I all too often align myself with people who are – or who I want to be – close to me. I try to be an easy company. I help, support, remind. As if these actions would improve my chances of being accepted. Instead, I become useful and others use me, and when I stop doing that, they discipline or reject me. Wrong! You can't buy being liked. You create bonds not by accommodating, but by holding your place. The bonds remain despite the fact that you are yourself or just because of it. Giving and taking this space during short evenings has created a sense of community and genuine joy of staying together.

Today I'm a little sad after saying goodbye, or maybe because this mountain was so exhausting... May your road ahead from here be easy for you!

Santiago – Negreira

DISTANCE 21,1 km
NUMBER OF STEPS 34,233

- How do you manage being yourself with others?
- When do you want to accommodate so as not to disturb or stay?
- How can there be more of you when you are others?
- How to end relationships in which you are only useful?

NOTES

VIVA LA FIESTA

22 lipca 2022

I love naked men, and back to the poles, but let's take it one thing at a time

I left the angelic alberga (srsly!), but it remained divine until the end of the road. No sun today, up to 20 degrees and the wind. A nice change.

I've had two lessons learnt:

1. On the trail, I met a group of young people. Young people can piss you off. They walk effortlessly, no backpacks, talking loudly. I was unhappy to see them come and pass me by. I was relieved when they overtook me and disappeared in front of me. When I got to the tea stop, they had all been already there. Can you guess

my reaction? Pure happiness it wasn't. But everything gets perverse here. After a while they started singing in parts, beautifully. Both female and male voices and parts. They sang: Viva la fiesta. I started humming along and a moment later I set out singing Viva la fiesta aloud and hopping. It's the kind of song that can make your day. 5 km later it turned out that I left my poles in the bar. They already wanted to stay earlier, because after my morning coffee I had to go back to get them. So I had no poles and no Angel left. Maybe I don't need them anymore? Maybe I can go on alone? I love 'Throw it away' by Aga Zaryan. But the poles followed me back. A few hours later, a friend from the Angelic alberga brought them to me. How did he know? How did it happen? They'll probably come in handy. Today I had no problem walking without them.

- Maybe leaning on someone or something for too long limits us?
- Maybe you can do without them, which is better for you?
- What helped you in the past and is now limiting your options?
- What and who do you think you can't do without?
- But what if you can?

2. I find naked men very attractive! No suits, no positions, no pecking order... I've been meeting here men who are honest, sensitive, aware both of themselves and what they're here for. I haven't met any warriors, defenders of the faith, brave breadwinners or tough cookies. Only those who cared for their children, women, wives, and parents. They were looking for the right way to reach them. They didn't flex their muscles. They weren't sure they could make it. At the same time, I can't remember ever feeling as good and safe as in their company. It was nice to see them get emotional when they were talking about their problems. I had no desire to help or change them. They were beautiful in their openness.

- Why do men find it so hard to be in touch with themselves on a daily basis?
- Is it that our and their expectations turn them into plastic heroes, afraid of where they stand compared to others?
- What can you do to give space to the men you care about so that they can connect with each other and not feel pressured to be different?
- Is this intimacy possible in a world full of expectations?

Less than 50 km to Fisterra. I leave the props that I don't need and the expectations of men that destroy rather than build them. **What are you going to leave?**

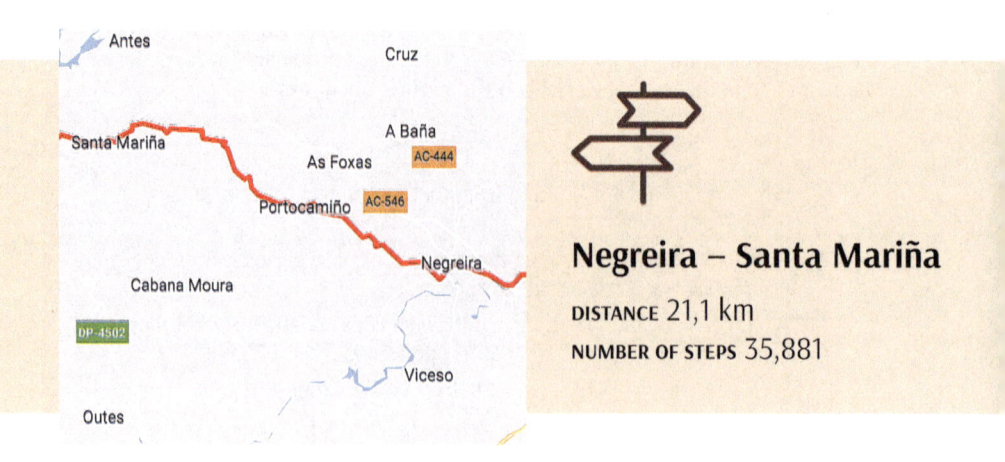

Negreira – Santa Mariña

DISTANCE 21,1 km
NUMBER OF STEPS 35,881

NOTES

13 STOPOVERS

July 24, 2022

When you watch people move around the alberga, you want to refer them to two places: to a rehabilitation ward and to a psychiatric ward (these are the ones who can barely walk and still enjoy it)

But between 5 a.m. and 7 a.m. they set off on another 20-30 km trek. Why? It's stopovers that turn the traveller into a cripple. Once you warm up, you can walk confidently without limping. This is the wisdom of the road. Even though you need a break, it doesn't pay to take it too often. If it's only for a moment, just tread in place, to keep the muscles warm. I like to rest too much. Each warm-up costs more energy. I take my obligatory rest after work every day, but later on I don't feel like doing anything at all. I need to make better use of the warm-up, tread during breaks and rest only when I need to, not just in case. Getting started is the hardest, especially after a long break, but then it gets easier. The hardest part is to get going.

Today, a reward for 15 km of walking non-stop. Medieval festival: bagpipes, stalls, locals dressed in medieval costume. This is the second dose of emotion at the sight of the ocean again today. Finally it was downhill.

15 km to Fisterra. Get your stones ready, which is to say:
your regrets, unforgiven losses, responsibility for others and everything that weighs on you. Today or tomorrow we'll unload our life burdens. It all depends on where I'm going to take a break.

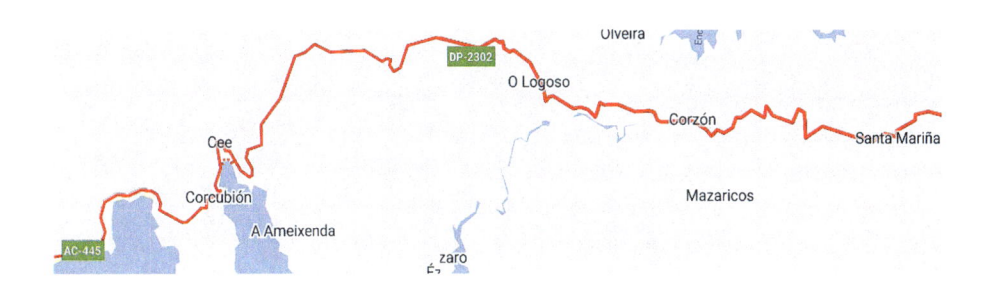

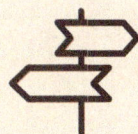

Santa Mariña – Hopital

DISTANCE 29,7 km
NUMBER OF STEPS 51,641

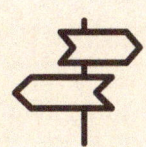

Hopital – Playa de Estorde

DISTANCE 20,8 km
NUMBER OF STEPS 36,830

- What are you putting off to get started?
- How not to give up after the first few steps?
- When should you rest and when should you push forward during the warm-up?

NOTES

14 UNLOADING THE BURDEN

July 25, 2022

The fog is coming down

Out of the clouds and the murmur of the waves emerges the sea with the fishermen's boats and the town of Fisterra. You go to Fisterra to die. To shed everything that has accumulated, stuck or been chosen out of fear or ill-gotten ambition (although it is probably the same as fear...). You go to Fisterra to see the vastness of the ocean of possibilities. To feel free.

In the evening I will go where the headland ends. I will throw away the stone that I've been carrying all these 400 km. I'll burn the things that I no longer need as the sun will be going down. I'll look at the ocean of stars. Do the same. You can burn the list of burdens or throw it away together with a symbolic stone. I will not do it for you, but I'm glad that you are ready to get rid of one thing or another.

The sun goes down in Fisterra at 22:06. You can join me at the same time. I'll feel more at ease together. I feel like it's going to be the happiest funeral I'll ever have a chance to attend.

Thank you for your presence, my friends on the journey of self-exploration!

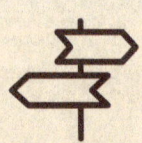

Playa de Estorde – Fisterra

DISTANCE 10,3 km
NUMBER OF STEPS 20,707

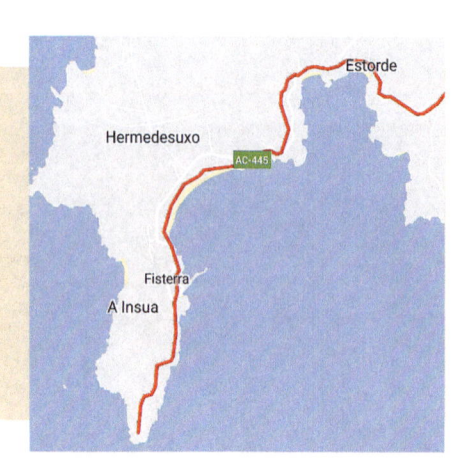

- What is your biggest burden?
- Which attitude limits you?
- What is it like to live without guilt, shame or fear?
- What can you give up to feel joy and peace every day?
- How would you feel rocking in God's cradle?

NOTES

15 FUNERAL AT THE END OF THE WORLD

July 26, 2022

Now that's what I call a funeral!

Enter the bagpipes and 'Besame mucho' played on the harp. The mystery play of the setting sun, dolphins parading right by the shore, scouts holding pennants, and the murmur of the wind and waves. The tourist buzz has died down. The burdens can feel honoured by leaving with dignity, and not just any old how. Whatever they were, I gave them time and space. It's as if you wanted to go to a new school without saying goodbye to the teachers from your previous stage in life. Not all of them were fantastic, most weren't fabulous, but yet they were there...

By choosing them, I have invited them into my life. I understand development differently today. More like getting rid of illusions in your life. Beneath them is the truth. Between illusion and truth lies disappointment. Why not celebrate it, if it brings us closer to who we are? Yesterday I celebrated the death of illusion. Illusion and magic sound ephemeral and deceptive, but they make us carry our burdens.

Let those come forward who threw/burned/washed them away (delete as appropriate).

Fisterra – Santiago

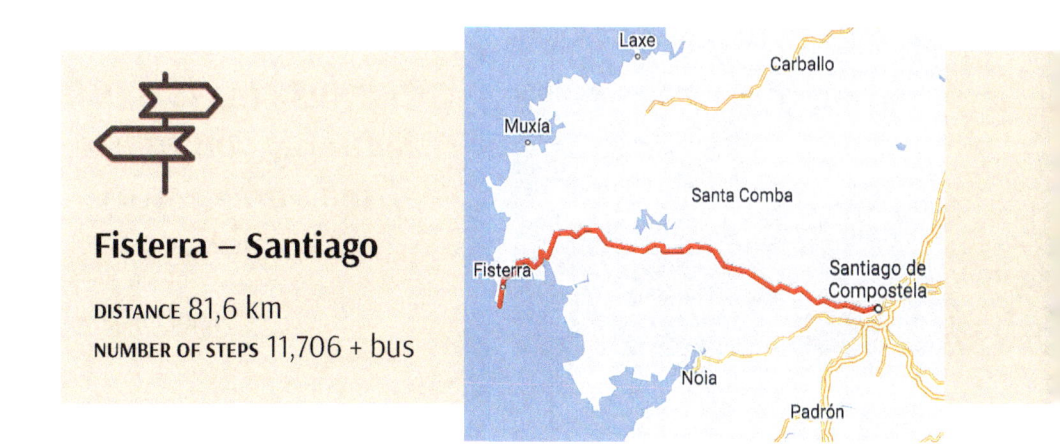

DISTANCE 81,6 km
NUMBER OF STEPS 11,706 + bus

The road teaches you how to keep your feet firmly on the ground even when your mind is soaring. To make dreams come true. Guaranteed success in harmony with yourself. Right for you in size, speed and form. Joy and peace.

> **Your heart gets much lighter if you free it from unnecessary illusions.**
>
> **Author unknown**

- How does it feel to say goodbye to your illusions?
- What is it like to build life on real premises?
- What is it like to let go and forgive yourself for indulging in magic and fantasy for a while?

NOTES

6 CLAM

July 26, 2022

This is the end of this stage of my journey of self-exploration

Do I have a better idea who I am? Yes! I have the structure of a shell or clam. The shell covers me outside. It has its own colour and rough texture. Some may like it, others don't. It may look different depending on the sun, wind and waves, the purity of the water and the type of soil. That is the self that I know and you know it too. It's pretty tough, ready to defend itself if anything happens. But my shell also has an inner lining. Smooth, shiny, and calm. That's the self that you know less or not at all. It hides my secrets, thoughts, and experiences. It is from this part that I write these posts. But best of all, I still have shell spirit! It tickled the inside of me all the way. It opened and closed the shell. It was having a great time. It would throw out sand, excess salt and seaweed from the inside to let new views in... I don't know it well. It is me and at the same time it is something more. It doesn't need my shells, it transcends them. You get to know the spirit from the side of this inner smoothness. The outer roughness has no access to the spirit. Clams are wrapped by the sea and given everything they need. But if a shell believes that it is only the outer part, its spirit may feel unnecessary. It will open the shell and swim to a place where it can tickle some other tender inside. The shell will break apart and waves will throw it ashore. Walking along the beach you will see shells with their inside and outside facing the sun, but without their spirit. Then you will remember how important it is to connect with your delicate inner self. You will preserve your spirit, which, hopefully, will be as witty and busy as mine on the Camino.

Ultreia! This is how they greet people who come to Santiago. Yesterday I felt like Catherine the Great. The king came to Santiago for my return and there were concerts. He didn't need to. I made the most of fresh octopus (no recording, please!) and a decent big band concert. There is much to celebrate, but at the same time fatigue is starting to get to me. Today is the day of return.

The journey of self-exploration never ends. Many people are back on the trail. I have returned to myself and I will not let it go. This is the best date of my life. Naturally, after death there will be time for rebirth. I hope you will be with me then.

> ❝ *Happiness is a feeling that comes from within, only you can decide about your happiness.* ❞
>
> **Author unknown**

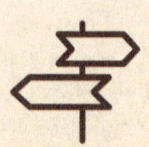

Santiago – Warszawa

DISTANCE 3,076 km
NUMBER OF STEPS 8,077 + plane

- What is your structure?
- How do you reach your inner self?
- How does it feel?
- How do you nurture your spirit?
- What happens if you forget about it?
- How much time do you reserve for your inner self?

NOTES

7 COMING BACK

July 29, 2022

Legs can have some rest

I haven't lost weight (oh!), but I've toned up. But there's still some work for the head to do. Warsaw is a place for hard shells. Will I find a place for myself here in the new look? What tasks will be there for me and which won't happen again? Can they be accomplished from the position of my inner self? I don't know. But I am ready to change to give the open heart its own big space in my everyday life. What doesn't help will go away, leaving room for what's right for me. I'm happy and curious to see how it goes. Now it's time to find my own path on the Camino of life. I hope to see the first pointers soon.

I'm very grateful that I had space to make this trip. That's why I would like to thank my teams at BizYou and Lu-BI Outsourcing HR for their professionalism, independence and entrepreneurial spirit. I was able to set off on my journey knowing that my cat would have good company and loving care, courtesy of Ania Lorenc, Szymon Lorenc, Zosia, Franek and Piotr, Lucyna and Leszek and Ela. Piotr Moreno was kind enough to offer his technical assistance. I am very grateful to all of you!

Special thanks to Ewa Rzodkiewicz for teaching me how to use the trekking poles and to Małgorzata Stocka for helping me choose the equipment for the expedition.

I was amazed at how much support I received from those closest to me and that when I told you what I was going to do, you said: Cool! Great idea! Nobody said it was crazy. It was the ultimate expression of trust. Bigger than that I had for myself and the idea. You are really fantastic!

I have tried to thank everyone who cheered me on, shared their thoughts and supported me. You have no idea how important this was, especially at the moments when my strength was failing. I know that I have many good friends and well-wishing companions among you. You can count on me on your travels!

People are always part of our camino. The better we get along with ourselves, the better we get along with others.

I had no idea I had so many friends on my journey of self-exploration.

> *Be the change you want to see in the world.*
>
> **Mahatma Gandhi**

- Who do you share your innermost plans and ideas with?
- Who cheers you on and supports you?
- Who helps you prepare for the next stage?
- Who takes care of your support base?
- Who do you want to thank?
- Who can you call when you're losing strength?

NOTES

8 ULTREIA!

August 11, 2022

Ultreia means 'we keep walking on'

I came back from the trail to my life's Camino. What are the lessons for today?

The first is time. **You have to give yourself time for everything that's important**. I made time in the morning and holidays came. Then I found myself as I am. I feel a deep connection with myself. I love myself unconditionally. My successes and failures don't matter. My spirit is joyful, affectionate and zesty. I love it! But without those time pills, nothing would have happened. In the professional area either. I'm giving up more roles and tasks. I'm making room for what's new. I'm dreaming about directions for the future. And it will come. Maybe it has already arrived. I have an unusual proposition. As if custom-made for me. It fits even better than the one I had in mind. We'll see if it's really for me. But I can think about it because I have made room and time for new things. Too often I have tried to hold on to the old and change at the same time. It didn't work... Decisions to make room are important. Perhaps the most important. **You can't be on both banks of the river at the same time**. You have to cross it or build a bridge.

- Does it take time?
- What do you need to make room for in your life?
- How much time will you reserve?
- How will you earmark it?
- How will you make others respect this time?
- What will you have to let go?
- What decisions will you need to make to make room for new things?
- What is waiting for you across the river?
- How will you say goodbye to the riverbank you are standing on?

NOTES

The second lesson learnt is **staying in the energy of the heart**.

I have learned to do everything the cold way, to the point where I almost froze to death. I warmed up on the road. The heart is hot. But habit is our second nature. **I need to make sure that I start every activity by remembering the heart**. First heart, then email. First, heart then talk. First heart, then put a slice of tomato on the sandwich. When I bear it in mind, everything is new and fresh as for a Camino. When I forget about it, I feel nothing. I'm freezing. I want to stay alive. On the trail I learned to distinguish between the condition of the outer shell and the cheerful snail inside. I see it in myself and in others. My conversations with others have changed. Sometimes they are deeper, sometimes happier. Perhaps you can only connect with others once you connect with yourself? I was wrong to think that I could survive by hiding and exposing my shell. I almost died. I only live naked. By discovering the soft part I am alive and safe. I was wrong to think otherwise. It's good to change your mind in time.

- What is your way to feel the energy of your heart?
- How do you want to remember it?
- How to trust that you can survive with your heart on your sleeve?
- When will you try it out?

Another lesson learnt. Lest the picture be too rosy, I have a few loose ends to tie up. I scratched the right side of my car just after I got home, and yesterday I added another scratch for good measure when I bumped into a hydrant put up ad hoc by Warsaw Waterworks without any warning signs. Good thing that it's only one side! Just before my departure, I began to polish the side by rubbing against the garage wall. I don't know yet what lesson it was supposed to be, but I'm looking forward to learning it. It will be much safer for the cars I drive. Evidently I need to change something in that area. **With myself I will succeed!**

NOTES

SUMMARY

It's been an extraordinary time for me. I'm happy it's not over yet. I'm happy not to be back to normal. I won't be back. There's no point. In addition to writing down this adventure, I hope to be ready to prepare a more structured plan of the journey of self-exploration. Perhaps one day I can guide others along such routes. Still I need to give it some more time and space.

If you are here with me, I want to thank you for your trust. I hope you're already holding yourself by the hand, or will soon.

Please share your journey with me as I have shared mine. Write to me and to your loved ones to inspire them. You can send them this e-book if you find it helpful. I believe that the more people are in happy contact with each other, the better the world will be. Our stories contribute to building a joyful and tender reality and offer an alternative to those who also hear the call to explore themselves.

I hope that one day our paths will cross and before we each go our own way at our own pace, we will feel the magic of being part of the Camino family. **Where everyone walks alone, but is never lonely**.

Bom caminho!

> *If you can dream it,
> you can do it.* ""

Walt Disney

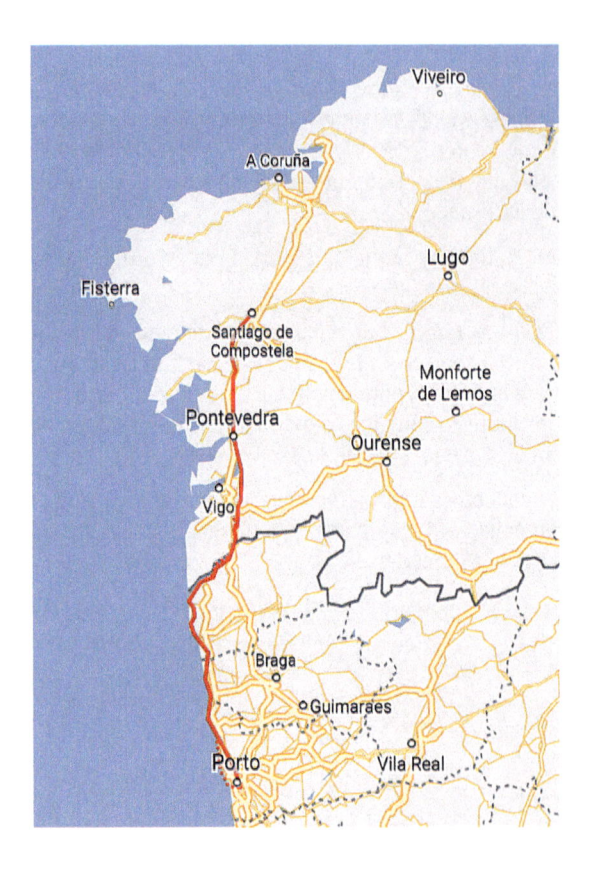

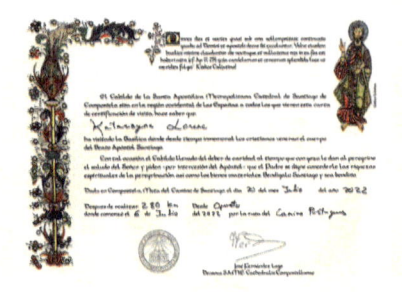

REVIEWS

Marzena Myszkowska

coach
lifecoach
change and mindfulness coach

Patterns and stereotypes built into us from childhood all too often do not let us understand and discover ourselves. Also, and most importantly, we fail to understand and explore our needs that are lost in the rush of life's demands. We form, create and build our standard of living through scripts uploaded to us by the environment (family, school, friends, etc.) from an early age. But then there comes a moment when we feel 'our shoes have become too tight for us'. Only when we take them off, we begin to see our needs. We discover ourselves in our own space of life. This space has been beautifully explored by Kate. Overcoming one's weaknesses, not only physical but also emotional, is quite a challenge. She did a great job discovering them on her journey – some for the first time. Physically and spiritually, this journey has set new paths in her life. The force with which crossed miles of unknown space has set a new vector for her further journey of self-discovery. The challenge she took on is surprisingly brave. But do we have time other than the time we have?

Kate, I believe that this is your best time. I congratulate you for respecting your own life and finding what you feel, rather than what the environment demands of us. A beautiful step towards opening up to yourself and the world.

Weronika Laura Ławniczak

founder and owner of
Holispace Instytut

I admire the inner beauty of human beings. I love to see people grow and receive abundance, and shape their personalities. Humbly accepting the prize will take them to a place where 'more' means less. When you get off the couch and feel close to yourself, in touch with the elements of Mother Nature, you will inevitably find peace of mind, well-being and joy as you take the path of inner evolution.

When you set off for Santiago, Kate, I went with you in the intention of leading. I felt joy and sadness in the different tones of colour and vibration. When you choose to meet yourself, you will meet your shadow in a different guise each day. You tame it, take it as it is and tuck it in. You can unleash its power and double the strength of your being. It is humanly impossible to digest

in everyday life. When we cross the gate of courage – we reach out for it, just like you did; returning often brings no joy, for you want more. More and less at the same time. The less the more... You have taken what is yours, you have taken the power, and no one will understand how much you have carried, how much you have gained. (From my diary)

Jarosław Olszewski

homo sapiens I human I hombre I
男人

Camino de Santiago is addictive. This Way is an end in itself. It is the time to think things over, to calm down, and to look inside your soul. Anyone who has experienced it knows. I highly recommend it to everyone: regardless of their religion, race, age or beliefs.

Alicja Biłozor

psychotherapist
Gestalt

What would be worth my Camino?

This question has made the greatest impression on me and took me on the longest journey. It faced me with fundamental questions about my values and my own Camino. My Camino has turned out to be every road I discover within myself in a new, previously inaccessible way. A road that spares no effort, but draws a hitherto unknown landscape. I followed Kate's journey almost from the beginning, eagerly awaiting and relishing each new post, and treating the questions like dessert. They made me pause and were a source of inspiration. Feelings of admiration mixed with envy, words were read with reflection. It's great to be called, but it's even greater to follow the voice. Thank you, Kate.

Anna Lorenc

intellectual disabilities teacher
visual impairment teacher

We do not travel to escape life. We travel so that life does not escape us. If you dream of the Camino but, like me, haven't yet set off on it, I cordially invite you to embark on this journey from the comfort of your armchair. Join Kate, who will take you on a journey of self-exploration in an unusual way and with great sensitivity. You'll have the opportunity to get to know yourself better, more deeply, and with more sensitivity, so that your dreams and needs don't get lost in our reality of time pressures, deadlines and noise.

Agnieszka Marta Maruda

leadership mentor
business trainer
speaker

A wise and insightful story about a journey from head to heart. An expedition for a relationship with oneself and with the world. On the one hand, very physical, and on the other – totally metaphysical and transformative. Maybe not everyone will choose the physical Camino, but everyone has a chance to experience their metaphysical Camino with Kate thanks to the content and questions contained in this e-book. It goes so well that even the smallest rhymes begin to swell – Camino and Kate excel! It's a pretty good concept to choose, feel, and experience for yourself. As long as you do something in addition to reading.

Look into Kate's quest and there is a chance that you will see yourself.

Marzena Mazur

business psychologist
speaker
mentor
editor of the 'Boss Zone' at TokFM Radio

Sometimes we don't go on a journey because we fear failure, and sometimes because we don't have company. Kate Lorenc has not only made the journey of getting to know herself, but she has also created a guide for those who find it difficult to embark on the same path of self-discovery. Her book offers support and companionship on a journey that takes everyone to a different place. She asks questions with understanding and love and patiently seeks answers. She leads by the hand those who didn't know how to start, and offers protection to those who are already on their way. Thanks to this book, the author – like a tender guide – accompanies us at every stage of getting to know ourselves.

Ewa Rzodkiewicz

entrepreneur
memeber of the Board of Directors of
    the Association of Professional Speakers
director of the Warsaw Lodge of
    Business Centre Club

'My Camino' is my Camino. I was there with Kate, preparing for the trip, teaching her how to walk with trekking poles, supporting her. And then I went on a journey with her not literally but spiritually, on a journey of self-exploration.

Her travelogue posts are not an ordinary diary, they set the azimuth, they are the compass on the journey of life. Today I read these words again and I read them as if I had written them myself, I discover them in words, in statements, and I keep asking myself questions about myself.

Everyone has their own way to walk on the Camino. You don't have to go abroad, just be prepared to leave your thousand roles behind for a while, be prepared to forget for a moment who you are, ask yourself questions and look for the right answers. Dare to embark on a journey into yourself.

Marianna Bartke

Theta Healing Master

I am very impressed with Kate's journey. I admire her insight, her ability to set goals and her self-observation, while the wonderful photographs, which made me feel as if I was with her on this journey, added to the appeal. I'm filled with admiration.

Kate has a talent for using words to immortalize her experiences, which is why I recommend this publication.

Grażyna Sroczyńska

entrepreneur
mentor
member of the Business Centre Club Convention
Digital Transformation Expert

> I think everyone has a moment in their life when they realise they're not walking their own path in this world, but someone else's. This is because we live in a culture that, at every turn, shows us and even dictates how we should function and adapt to the world. 'How to live' books are still very popular; parents plan their children's careers from an early age; social media promote an ideal world and create a comparison effect that is destructive and toxic like no other.
>
> Everyone around you knows how to live and which way to go. So what is it all for? As a result, cortisol floods our bodies, and instead of feeling the joy of success, we really just feel relief. And that's not what these guides are about, is it?

Anna Urbańska

Master Trainer
STRUCTOGRAM® Poland

When I first heard that Kate was on her way to Santiago, I felt that it was time for me to travel, to find myself. From the beginning of the year I was stuck in my huge 'I DON'T KNOW'. I don't know who I am, what I want, where am I going.

Your journey, Kate, has also been a powerful experience for me, through which I have learned and understood a great deal.

My main conclusions:

1. Everything I need is inside me and I already have it.
2. In silence, solitude, wandering, you can hear yourself better, more clearly, and everything seems to be sharper.
3. It can be seen how much strength and power we have when we wrestle not with business, others, money, clients, but with ourselves.
4. We can find yourself only when we are ready for it. Trying to force yourself to search just because you have to won't work.
5. Beauty is in the journey, not in its destination.

I am grateful to you, Kate, for her journey. For leaving your and my intentions behind. For who you are and for daring to show us who we are as you see it. May all be well for you.

Thank you!

ABOUT THE AUTHOR

Kate Lorenc

CEO of HR organisations, coach and mentor to organisational leaders, Business Centre Club (the oldest and most prestigious organisation of entrepreneurs participating in Poland's economic transformation) expert on the labour market and management efficiency, vice-president of the Provincial Labour Market Council, member of the Business Centre Club Convention, representative of employers in the Sectoral Council of Trade Competences and the Council of Stakeholders of the Integrated Qualifications System, president of TOP HR Group, initiator and Chairperson of the Jury of the Employee of the Year competition. Until 2022, she was the vice-president of Business Centre Club and the vice-chancellor of the BCC Warsaw Lodge, member of the labour law team of the Social Dialogue Council.

An economist by training, she specialises in economic policy and entrepreneurship strategy. She completed post-graduate course in contemporary philosophy. Kate has received several awards from the Social and Economic Committee of the European Union for the high quality of her services, e.g. for leading organisations through change, as well as competence and organisation diagnosis. Today, her companies provide services to more than 200 companies in total. She is a master trainer in researching and developing mental toughness, resilience and leadership effectiveness. She educates and certifies HR professionals, trainers and coaches in psychometric and diagnostic tools. She has conducted one of the the first in Europe research study on the strength and resilience of employees and management style, and regularly surveys the European labour market and monitors the implementation of remote and hybrid working.

Her hobbies include is sailing, walking, personal and spiritual development.

NOTES

NOTES

NOTES

Printed in Great Britain
by Amazon